Lanzarote

EVEREST

Text: Bartolomé Egea

Photography: Oliviero Daidola
              Paolo Tiengo
              Justino Díez

Lay out: Francisco Bargiela

Cover design: Alfredo Anievas

Translation: EURO:TEXT

© EDITORIAL EVEREST, S.A.
Carretera León-La Coruña, km 5 - LEÓN
ISBN: 84-241-3575-X
Legal deposit: LE. 151-1997
Printed in Spain

EDITORIAL EVERGRÁFICAS, S.L.
Carretera León-La Coruña, km 5
LEON (Spain)

The **island of Lanzarote** (also known by the nickname *Isla de los Volcanes* or *Island of Volcanoes*) is completely covered by over 100 volcanoes, volcanic craters and fields of petrified lava. The slopes and peaks of its low mountains are covered in black volcanic soil.

Lanzarote divides neatly into two distinct areas: the first, to the south-east and north-east of the island, is the area shaped by volcanic eruptions of over 3,000 years ago, such as the eruption of the **Corona volcano,** which gave rise to the area now known as the Malpaís de la Corona and to the great volcanic tunnel in which **Jameos del Agua** and **Cueva de los Verdes** are found. But it was the series of volcanic eruptions which took place between 1730 and 1736 that endowed the island's typical lunar landscape with its most distinctive features. These eruptions shaped the volcanic area now known as the **Timanfaya National Park,** located in the central-western part of the island. April 1st, 1730 heralded the beginning of what we could describe as the greatest known volcanic holocaust. Thirty-two volcanoes rose up like hell itself from the entrails of the earth, spewing forth huge quantities of molten rock, thereby creating that incomparable expanse of lava which today constitutes the island's most important attraction. Beneath these mountains, craters and lava deserts lies, forever silent, what remains of the villages of Tingafa, Mancha Blanca, Maretas, Santa Catalina, San Juan, Peña de Palmas, Timanfaya, Tetegua and Rodeo, which were situated in what was the most fertile part of the island. There is a Spanish adage that goes *No hay mal que por bien no venga* (There is no ill out of which some good does not come), and this saying is certainly true of the island of Lanzarote, as the events of the 17th and 18th centuries which brought ruin to its inhabitants have today become the main reason behind its attraction as a tourist destination, thus bringing wealth and well-being to the descendents of those who suffered the volcanic destruction.

The island of Lanzarote (or *Titeroi-Gatra* as it appears to have been called by its early inhabitants before the island was conquered by the Norman Jean de Béthencourt on behalf of the Castilian crown in 1402) is the most northerly of the Canary Islands and is 68 miles from the African coast and 1,000 miles from the Spanish mainland.

The island of Lanzarote is completely covered by over 100 volcanoes.
Different sights of the island:
Page 3: Teguise, fron the Santa Bárbara castle.
Pages 4 and 5: Yaíza.
Page 7: Graciosa Island, from the Río Lookout.

Until fairly recently, agriculture, fishing and its by-products were its inhabitant´s only sources of income.

*Parrots at
Guinate Tropical Park.*

Arrecife Port. ➤

Together with Fuerteventura and the small islets of **Lobos, La Graciosa, Alegranza, Montaña Clara, Roque del Este** and **Roque del Oeste,** it forms the group of islands known as the *eastern islands.* Lanzarote has a surface area of 795 square kilometres, which makes it the fourth-largest of the Canary islands. Lanzarote's north-eastern coastline is fairly rugged, but in the south-east there are many fine beaches. The climate is mild, with average temperatures oscillating between 18° C to 24° C all year round. It rains infrequently, with an annual average figure of about 200 mm. The vegetation is clearly xerophilous (adapted to a sunny, dry climate) and the island's most typical tree is the Canarian palm tree, which is particularly abundant in the **Haría valley.** Lanzarote's most characteristic feature is its volcanic landscape, which has earned it the nickname of *Isla de los Volcanes (Island of Volcanoes).* Until fairly recently, agriculture, fishing and its by-products and some shepherding were its inhabitant's only sources of income. Today, the influx of tourists to the island has completely transformed its economy, as the demand for services inspired by the tourist boom has enabled the island's inhabitants to leave their arid fields and find a better livelihood in the tourist areas.

At **Guinate Tropical Park,** situated in a singularly beautiful setting in the north of the island beside the *Mirador de Guinate* on the **Famara cliffs,** visitors can enjoy the surprising and amusing antics of parrots and cockatoos.

The **Virgen de los Dolores hermitage** (also known as the *Virgen de los Volcanes*) was built by the inhabitants of the village of **Tinajo** as an offering to the Virgin for her miraculous intercession during the volcanic eruptions of 1730-1736, when the river of lava which was bearing down on the village altered its course, thus saving the village from being buried by lava, a fate which befell many of the neighbouring villages. The hermitage was opened for worship in the year 1781. The feast of the Virgen de los Dolores, which is very popular throughout the island, is celebrated on 15th September each year.

Arrecife Port.

Sunset in Arrecife. ➤

ARRECIFE

The **Charco de San Ginés,** a natural lake of calm waters whose level rises and falls along with the ocean tides, is connected to the sea via a small channel and is flanked by a modern avenue along three-quarters of its shores. It is used as a haven and mooring for light pleasure boats. The first buildings in Arrecife were built beside this lake, and the city's first church was also built nearby.

The **Castillo de San José,** situated overlooking Arrecife's harbour, was built on the orders of Carlos III to provide defence for the harbour and also to mitigate the famine which was affecting Lanzarote at the time, after a lack of rain for several years in a row had left the fields barren. For this reason it is also known as *El Castillo de Hambre (The Castle of Hunger).*

It has now been restored by the artist César Manrique, and is home to a museum of contemporary art with works by Picasso, Miró, César Manrique himself, and others.

Arrecife has magnificent parks and avenues built on land reclaimed from the sea, all of which have well-kept gardens and terraces from which strollers can gaze at the blue waters of the ocean and daydream about sailing in a pleasure boat over calm waters.

The **Puente de las Bolas,** a drawbridge dating from 1559, formed the entrance to the **Castillo de San Gabriel,** which was built on a small island facing the centre of the city in order to defend it from pirates and Saracens, who frequently attacked the island. The castle was first built in 1574. It was destroyed during successive invasions and was rebuilt and modernized in 1599 during the reign of Philip II. It now houses the archaeological museum.

Charco de San Ginés.

San Ginés church. ➤

San José Castle-Museum.

Museum of Contemporary Art inside of the San José Castle.

San Gabriel Castle.

Bolas Bridge, accesing the San Gabriel Castle.

The city of Arrecife seen from the San Gabriel Castle.

Fisherman's wharf in Arrecife.

The **Playa del Reducto** is in Arrecife itself, and is a beach of fine, clean white sand. Its transparent waters offer a year-round invitation to tourists and locals alike to dive in and enjoy Lanzarote's magnificent sun.

The view over **Arrecife** from the sea outside the city, with the attractive contrast between the whiteness of its buildings, the dark grey of the volcanic mountains and the blue of the ocean, will remain etched in your memory for a long time. The *church of San Ginés* (the patron saint of the city), which was the first church to be built in Arrecife, can be seen in the background.

Opposite: Farmland, Tinajo.

Natural fields of volcanic pebbles around **La Gería** shape one of Lanzarote's most beautiful and original landscapes.

Arrecife: General view and, below, Maritime Promenade.

La Geria: services and chapel of the Charity.

Windmill at Tinajo.

TINAJO AND YAÍZA

In the northern part of the island, around **Tinajo,** the countryside is a patchwork of geometrical plots of land, outlined by windbreaks. Onions, watermelons, melons, pulses and potatoes are the main crops, and are grown in artificial fields of volcanic pebbles. A layer of volcanic pebbles is spread over the earth in order to trap the humidity from the infrequent rainfall and the nightime dew.

Timanfaya National Park, which was formed during the volcanic eruptions between 1730 and 1736, has a unique beauty: it is an area of over 200 square kilometres consisting solely of a mass of craters and deep crevices. Great clumps of black sand cover the slopes and peaks of the mountains, as a reminder of the six year-long cataclysm which turned a fertile area into a veritable lunar landscape. Immense lava plains separate the mountains, rippled with indescribable abstract forms and strange bare assemblages of hieroglyphic stones. There is something Dantesque about contemplating this inferno called Timanfaya, whether you tour the park on the back of a camel or by some other means of transport.

At the spot known as **Islote de Hilario** in the *Mountains of Fire* the highest underground temperatures in the whole Timanfaya National Park are recorded. Temperatures of 400° C can be reached simply by gently scraping the surface of the ground. If water is poured into a small hole in the ground, enormous geysers of steam shoot out at high pressure and if any inflammable material is pushed into the ground, it bursts into flames instantly.

Timanfaya National Park.

Timanfaya National Park; vegetation.

Timanfaya National Park.

At the highest point in the Mountains of Fire is the Islote de Hilario, where the highest tempreetures are recorded. Temperatures of 400º C can be reached simply by gently scraping the earth.

Lanzarote has always had a great maritime tradition, with particular emphasis on fishing. Salt was required to supply the boats that went to fish along the African coast, so natural lakes along the island's coast were turned into saltworks. One of the most important surviving examples is the **Janubio saltworks** in the **Yaíza** area, which is also marvellous to look at, with the mountains of salt contrasting with the dark earth against the backdrop of the ocean.

El Golfo, situated on the western side of the island, is a group of truncated mountains of volcanic origin which resembling a semicircular Roman amphitheatre, dates from the volcanic eruptions of 1730-1736. TThe mountainsides display an array of colours resulting from their natural *architecture.* At the foot of the split cone which forms the amphitheatre is a small emerald green lagoon, whose waters filter in from the ocean through the stretch of volcanic earth that separates the two.

Close by are the *hervideros* (*boiling waters*), which are known by this name due to the fact that as the rough sea crashes against the reefs formed by the rivers of lava that once ran into the sea, huge mountains of white foam are created. Together with the colourful coastline and the roar of the waves they are a marvellous spectacle.

The **Santa Sport** sports and tourist resort is a complex of apartments situated by the sea near Tinajo in the north of the island and has marvellous salt-water swimming pools which are connected to the sea. Its complete range of sports facilities are the best on the island, and attract athletes from all over Europe and America (especially Scandinavia) who come both to train and relax as, apart from the magnificent beaches already mentioned, there are also leisure facilities, shops and modern, comfortable apartments.

Yaíza.

The Janubio Saltworks.

El Golfo. ➤

El Golfo. Beach.

Los Hervideros. (Hot springs).

Laguna Verde. El Golfo.

▼ *Santa Sport.*

Waiting for the ferry.

▼ *Playa del Papagayo.*

Las Coloradas Castle.   Punta del Papagayo. ➤

The **Castillo de las Coloradas,** which guards the **La Bocayna Strait** (the arm of sea situated between the islands of Lanzarote and Fuerteventura), was built in the year 1742. Shortly afterwards it was burned and destroyed by pirates who invaded this part of the island in search of slaves and livestock. It was later rebuilt and modernized during the reign of Carlos III, and is now a national monument. It is a two-storey circular building with an Isabelline style belltower. Magnificent views over the **Islet of Lobos** and the coast of Fuerteventura are obtained from the roof.

Femés: typical house and church.

Uga is an agricultural village built on what was once buried by lava from the volcanic eruptions between the years 1730 and 1736. Not very far away, **Femés,** a village belonging to the Yaíza municipality and located on the massif of Los Ajaches. From this massif, there are a number of cliffs toward the coast. All of them are cut out by a platform, giving way to the formation of the many coves that form the so called *Papagayo Beach.*

The church of **Femés,** with completely smooth walls, is built in the same place where the cathedral of San Marcial de Rubicón was found, until it was destroyed in the XVI century by English pirates. From this point a road takes us to the Papagayo beaches and the small fishermen's wharf on *Blanca Beach.*

Above: Church of Uga and surrounding view. Below: goat farmer.

Playa Blanca.

Lanzarote is the ideal place to practice water sports.

Playa Blanca. ➤

The church and square at San Bartolomé.

Tías. ➤

Puerto del Carmen.

Around Teguise.

Market Day in Teguise.

Old police station.

Palacio Espínola.

Teguise:
1.- Houses made of earth .
2.- Peasant.
3.- Cock fight.   4.- Church. ➤

Costa Teguise: Windmill and surfing.

Another view of Costa Teguise.

TÍAS AND SAN BARTOLOMÉ

The *parish church of San Bartolomé de Lanzarote* was built around 1799, and houses the figure of *St. Bartholomew,* the patron saint of the village, whose feast day is celebrated amid great popular enthusiasm every 24th August. Most of the inhabitants of the village are farm labourers, and the village is famous for its wines and cheeses. Its traditional group of serenaders is the most important on the island.

The **Puerto del Carmen** tourist development has been built with great aesthetic sensitivity and is designed to blend harmoniously with its surroundings. Its low, uniform buildings are all painted white and gleam beneath the Canary sun. It is hard to say whether the buildings add to the beauty of the beaches or whether the beaches themselves, combined with the surroundings, are what makes this a sight that visitors will always remember with nostalgia.

All sorts of pleasure boats and sporting activities can be seen along Puerto del Carmen's four kilometres of beaches and coves, depending on which part of the coast you watch from. In some parts the strong waves attract windsurfers, and a wide range of other nautical sports are enjoyed in the calmer waters.

Tías, a district covering an area of 64 square kilometres, slopes gently from north to south and is flanked by some 9 kilometres of coastline, of which over 6 kilometres are stunningly beautiful beaches and coves with clean sand and transparent waters. Until a few years ago, Tías was the poorest area of Lanzarote and had very few inhabitants who, with superhuman effort, scratched precarious harvests consisting mainly of pulses, tomatoes and onions from the arid soil. Just a handful of houses were scattered among the different villages, although they were very picturesque with their white painted walls standing out in the sun against the volcanic blackness of the surrounding land.

Today, thanks to the tourism boom of the last few years, the district of Tías and its coastline have undergone a profound change, with an increase both in population and wealth. Puerto del Carmen is now the most important tourist resort on the island, both in terms of its infrastructure and wide variety of tourist accommodation and of its beaches with their innumerable terraces, discotheques, etc.

Puerto del Carmen has a small fishing harbour, which is also used to moor small pleasure boats. Locals call it **La Tiñosa,** the original name of the village which later became known as Puerto del Carmen after the coast was developed. This harbour, which is situated in the historic heart of the village, is a popular haunt of both locals and visitors alike at the times of day when the fishing boats are setting out and returning.

Puerto del Carmen's clean, white-sand beaches are the best on the island. **Playa Blanca** is the largest of these beaches and is bordered by a large avenue which is full of cafés, pubs and a wide variety of shops, which give it a fairground appearance during the day and a fantastical appearance at night owing to the streetlamps and multi-coloured lights.

The typical Lanzarote style of construction consists of straight lines, thick walls to keep the heat out, small exterior openings, white painted walls, decorative Turkish-style chimneys and doors and windows painted bright green, which perhaps reflects a yearning for the colour green in a landscape devoid of greenery. The contrast between the houses and the blackness of the surrounding land endows the landscape with great beauty. The rough waters of Lanzarote's north-eastern coast are ideal for windsurfing.

COSTA TEGUISE

Playa de las Cucharas in Costa Teguise is the largest and most important beach in the area, and is ideal for windsurfing (there is a windsurfing school here). Flanking the beach is the development of the same name, where the most important shopping centre in Costa Teguise is located. The development has been designed with a simple and attractive style of architecture to blend in with the volcanic surroundings. Nearby are the island's only golf course, aquatic amusement park and casino.

The dromedary is part of the Tías countryside. They say that it was introduced to the Islands by Spaniards who had brought them from the Sahara.

Monument to the Peasant in C. Manrique: images of the monument, of the restaurant (below) and of Sr. Brito working on his famous Canary figures.

Tahiche: César Manrique House-museum.

Costa Teguise's hotels are the most modern on the island and can rival the world's most famous hotels in facilities and comfort. Among them is the *Las Salinas hotel,* situated in a place known as **Playa del Charco.** It has been carefully designed to combine the arid, volcanic surroundings with a tropical atmosphere. Heads of state and other celebrities from all walks of life meet and stay in this hotel when visiting the island.

Apart from Costa Teguise's unsurpassable hotels and general infrastructure, there are also typical single-family residences surrounded by traditional patios full of well-kept flowers and black volcanic stone gardens. The volcanic stones fulfil two basic purposes: firstly, to create a harmonious contrast between their blackness and the white painted walls of the house and, secondly, to trap humidity in the garden, preventing the nightime dew from evaporating during the day.

The **Fundación César Manrique** is located in the house where the artist lived until 1987. Built on a lava outflow from the volcanic eruptions which devastated Lanzarote between 1730 and 1736, the latter has been extended and adapted to house the Foundation. Inside, structure and volume combine to create a marvellous space in which architecture and nature are harmoniously fused. The Foundation looks after and displays paintings, drawings, sculptures and other artefacts created by César Manrique.

The **Monument to the Peasant,** which stands outside San Bartolomé de Lanzarote, is a huge original sculpture by the local artist César Manrique and pays homage to the long-suffering peasants of Lanzarote. It is made of old cans of the kind that were once used to carry water. Next to the monument is an old, period-style mansion which has been converted into a peasant museum and restaurant serving a variety of typical local dishes.

El **Jardín del Cactus** (The Cactus Garden) is another creation of the Lanzarote-born artist, César Manrique. In a small space, the artist has managed to combine Lanzarote's extraordinary natural landscape with his own creativity. Over one thousand different species of cacti from all over the world have been planted

Tiagua Agricultural Museum.

together in a small area of land, in a beautiful setting whose inspiration is drawn from the forms of a Roman amphitheatre.

Visitors should not leave the island without touring this marvellous garden and contemplating the wide variety of species of all shapes and sizes. It will probably be one of the most unforgettable memories they take away from the island.

The Jardín del Cactus is in Guatiza, next to the road leading to another of Lanzarote's most popular sights: Jameos del Agua.

The **Chinijo archipelago,** as it is affectionately called by the natives of Lanzarote, is formed by the islands of **Graciosa, Montaña Clara** and **Alegranza** and the islets of **Roque del Este** and **Roque del Oeste,** all of which, with the exception of Isla Graciosa, are uninhabited. The inhabitants of Isla Graciosa are concentrated in a small village known as **Caleta del Sebo,** which stands beside a well-equipped fishing harbour, fishing being the livelihood of the majority of the islanders. Isla Graciosa has lovely large beaches, the best of which is known as the **Playa de las Conchas** (Shell Beach) because of the large numbers of shells which are to be found in the sand. Communication between Lanzarote and the Chinijo archipelago is channelled through the **Port of Orzola** and boats carrying passengers and merchandise leave and enter daily, crossing the small arm of sea (which locals refer to as a river) that separates Lanzarote and Isla Graciosa.

Haría could be defined as an oasis in the middle of Lanzarote. Situated in a dip surrounded by volcanic mountains, it is also known as 'the land of a thousand palm trees' due to the abundance of palm trees in

Cactus Park.

Graciosa Island, from Mirador del Río.

▼ Haría.

Orzola.

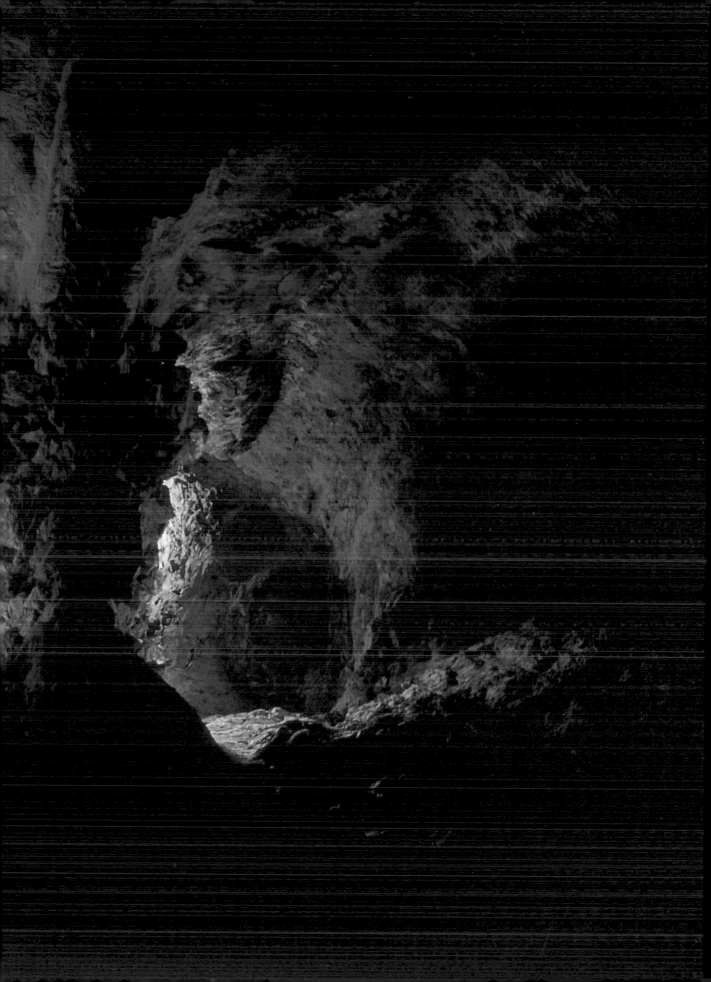

Cueva de los Verdes.

Jameos del Agua: Auditorium.

the valley. Even though the valley was razed by invading Saracen pirates in the not too far distant past, it still has the largest concentration of palm trees than anywhere else in the Canary Islands. The fertile Haría valley was the richest part of the island until the tourist boom drew its inhabitants away to other areas, the tourist industry offering a more secure and less arduous way of earning one's living than farming. The former splendour of the old ancestral homes can still be seen.

Playa de Famara, the longest beach in Lanzarote, is situated in the north of the island and is buffetted by the Trade Winds blowing off the Atlantic which makes it inhospitable and unsuitable for bathing. It is flanked by a series of small villas which are used as summer retreats by island residents. Part of the Chinijo archipelago can be seen from this part of the coast, and nearby are the rugged **Famara-Guatifay** mountains which are ideal for hang-gliding. This part of the coast is a popular place for underwater fishing.

Part of the great tunnel through which an immense river of lava from the Corona volcano flowed seawards over 3,000 years ago is known as **Cueva de los Verdes**. Over 6 kilometres long, 15 metres high and 15 metres wide, it is the largest volcanic tunnel yet discovered. Inside, an indescribably beautiful range of colour combinations can be seen.

This is where the early inhabitants of Lanzarote used to hide from pirates and Moors, who frequently invaded the island to capture and sell the natives as slaves.

The tunnel is now entered through a large, double-mouthed cave. Despite the fact that it is so long, only about two kilometres have so far been prepared to receive visitors.

Jameos del Agua contains a natural auditorium built in a bubble of lava which is a part of the volcanic tunnel described above.

It also contains a small, calm lagoon which is connected to the ocean through small underground galleries. The lagoon is home to a species of blind, albino crab which is unique to Lanzarote.

Two views of Jameos del Agua.

Images of a disappearing present: 1.- Peasant, near La Quemada,
2.- Old wine cellar El Grifo in the town of Masdache,
3.- Elderly woman from the town of Munique.